28 PITFALLS OF A MAN

A Practical Handbook Confronting
Traps Every Man Will Face

D1521159

Rodney Rankins Th. M

To order copies for Correctional Institutions, Non-Profit or Profit Organizations, Men's Ministries, County Jails, City Jails, Prison Ministries and Community Outreach Programs please visit: 28pitfallsofaman.com or send an email to: 28pitfallsofaman@gmail.com

Table of Contents

Prologue

Pitfall: A trap or snare, especially a roughly camouflaged pit, hidden or unrecognized danger.

28 Pitfalls is a personal journey of 28 of the pitfalls I have fallen into so many times and the daily struggle to stay out of them. By God's grace and putting in the work with it, we can avoid and even overcome as many as possible. We are solely responsible for everything we say and everything we do. For me, this 28 pitfalls journey is not about seeking sympathy or empathy, it's about accountability and self-awareness. Some of these pitfalls deal with character flaws, behaviors, patterns, traumatic even psychological issues but at the root of a lot of them, they are in essence spiritual and sinful. Whether it's believed or not, it's true—we will all give account of our lives before God. I've made my peace, repented for my sins, and welcomed Him to be Lord and Savior of my life. Working every day to not just be a better man but a better human being, period. Nobody wants to be remembered for the worst day of their life, for doing the worst thing they've ever done, but that's what could happen

when you fall into a pit. My pit was a real prison. Yours could be a metaphor—a figure of speech. Regardless of what your pit may be: mental, physical, emotional, spiritual, financial, or relationally, a pit is still the pits. Rock bottom. We should never cover up things that need to be uncovered. It's not easy to accept the fact that Jesus already overcame the same things we face daily, but it's true.

So come on, get ready to go on a journey, hopefully recognizing, addressing, and overcoming pitfalls in your own life as I share these particular 28 pitfalls with you.

Someone may even ask who do I think I am that qualifies me to think I can even write a book? My question is: who are you to not write one? An author I know is famous for saying "Don't die with your book still in you." Nobody can tell your story, your truth, the way you can. Don't leave it untold, concealed for speculation or hearsay. I definitely encourage you to share yours also, it may not be for you, who knows, it may be a game changer for someone else.

So, what's your story? Everyone has their own story to tell, it's called life, I'm just sharing a few things I've experienced in hopes to let someone else know they're not alone. It's a horrible feeling when that voice tells you you're the only one dealing with whatever it is that you're dealing with. From my experience, that would be the voice of shame saying that. It's a lie—you're not the only one, everybody's dealing with something. No matter what their zip codes are, what kind of car someone drives, the jewels they may have, whatever their status is, it doesn't matter what race they are or even what their faith is. We all deal with something. I'm saying this to remind you and myself that stuff happens to everybody. No one on the face of the earth is exempt. We're not the only ones.

I'm not an expert, my life and age has been what's given me over five decades of experience. I honestly feel compelled to share and help as many men as possible, whether they're in prison or out. There are a lot of innocent men in prison, just like there's a lot of guilty men who are walking around free. Again, we're all dealing with something. Be encouraged, we gotta keep moving forward. Whatever it is, we can get through it. God is faithful.

"Do not judge me by my successes, judge me by how many times I fell down and got back up again."

Nelson Mandela

Dedication

To my beautiful wife Tolliny of 30 years. I'm beyond blessed to have you as a great helpmate, best friend, partner, and so much more. You never gave up on me or us. I know I don't deserve you, I honestly don't think I would've made it without God keeping you in my life, I'm so grateful to still have you in my life. Despite everything. No words can ever express my love and gratitude for you. I'm forever indebted to you. I remember telling you over and over that I know I'm receiving the overflow of God's love, God's hands extended through you. You have given so much of yourself, I thank God for you; my virtuous Proverbs 31 woman—you're absolutely the greatest. I love you with all my heart, always.

Matthew 25:35-40 NIV

For I was hungry and you gave me something to eat, I was thirsty and you gave me something to drink, I was a stranger and you invited me in, I needed clothes and you clothed me, I was sick and you looked after me, I was in prison and you came to visit me. Then the righteous will answer him, 'Lord, when did we see you hungry and feed you, or thirsty and give you something to drink? When did we see you a stranger and invite you in, or needing clothes and clothe you? When did we see you sick or in prison and go to visit you?' "The King will reply, 'Truly I tell you, whatever you did for one of the least of these brothers and sisters of mine, you did for me.'

I relate to these verses from my heart, I'm one of the least of these brothers my King Jesus was referring to.

Pitfall 1

Dishonesty

Being dishonest is one of the many ways to end good things in our lives, from families, marriages, relationships, business deals, and anything we see as sacred or moral. When people feel that you're dishonest, it will limit trust and hinder what could've been a lifelong relationship on many levels. People will be reluctant to extend grace to you or anyone when they feel someone is being or has been dishonest. Practice truth at all costs, the truth will set us free.

Pitfall 2

Pride

I didn't realize that pride stops a person from growing. It will hinder spiritual and mental growth. Pride will keep you in a place of denial, delusion, and deception. It will make you believe you know it all and have everything all figured out.

The Bible says pride goes before the fall. I've had to deal with this one in ways I couldn't imagine. I was prideful and didn't know it. I lost just about everything I thought was important.

I'm sure, like so many other men and women too we think we know better or even have all the answers when we really don't. No one does. If you meet or know someone who has an answer for everything, beware that's a problem. Like I said I lost just about everything that I valued. An incredible twenty year plus marriage to the woman of my dreams, a successful career, community love and respect, relationships, beachfront condo, luxury cars, and a host of material things

I had worked for, all gone in a matter of days. My wife and I had built a successful sales business. After over twenty years in business we had semi-retired, moved to the beach and was working on starting a Ministry of helping others. All gone. God stayed right with me, though many times I didn't know it.

I was too mad at myself and Him, nobody ever wants to admit something like that, especially not someone who's a Christian. I'm sharing my truth, regardless of how hard it was to admit and honestly still is. I will tell you what my wife, who absolutely loves God, has faith to move mountains told me the reason she stayed with me as my friend was because she said "you never leave a wounded soldier on the front line, especially if they're still breathing." Man. You can drop the mic on that or real tears. That's the type of woman she is. Every time I think of that it reminds me of how much I'm loved. Anyway I was really starting to say what she always says that's absolutely true. She says "God is so faithful, full of grace and mercy, He always deals with us His children privately, before He deals with us publicly." I went from living on thousands of dollars a week to living on a few dollars a week and that was in commissary. I did not touch actual paper or coin currency for years. It's illegal and isn't used in prison. Everything is on your books, your in house account so to speak, all connected electronically to your inmate ID card. Money isn't allowed to be earned even with a job. I had to depend on family and friends every week to put money on my books. I learned a lot about trusting God during those times. He always remained faithful, even when I wasn't faithful and I didn't trust Him. Before prison for many years I was use to taking care of people, not being taken care of. I was brought down, humbled to my core. I'd been working and hustling since I was about 10 years old. It was a fast, painful, crazy, humiliating fall.

I alone take complete responsibility for this today and every day for the rest of my life and pray God's healing over all of us that have been impacted. Pride is no joke, it will derail a man, destroying not only him but anyone and everything around him.

Yet through it all I saw over and over God work miracles for me in spite of myself. I was no longer a provider, I saw Him be my provider through this very small number of faithful friends and family week after week, year after year. He became to me one of His many names, that name is Jehovah Jireh, it means God Provider. That's what He did for Abraham, He provided the sacrifice, the ram in the bush, check out Genesis 22 for the point of reference on Him being a Provider, specifically verse 14.

We have a great life example with King Nebuchadnezzar in the book of Daniel, start reading from chapter 1 to get the whole story, then by the time you get to the end of chapter 4 you'll see the epitome of what not only pride looks like but also the true mercy, redemption and restoration of Almighty God. It's humbling and amazing all in one. Check out what Proverbs 16:5 says, "The Lord detests the proud; they will surely be punished." Nebuchadnezzar's pride blinded him to the source of his success. Pray for humility, it's the exact opposite of being prideful.

Pitfall 3

Unforgiveness

Bitterness and unforgiveness will usually make you have ill feelings, sometimes for yourself but especially toward others. We know that God forgives, so we must forgive others, or should forgive because we've been forgiven, especially when we didn't deserve it. Many times, it's easier said than done. Regardless, forgiveness is a decision, not a feeling.

Unforgiveness, bitterness, and even anger have been linked to sickness, from a simple headache to terminal cancer—which is why doctors advise you to be optimistic. Try starting with forgiving yourself, sometimes people really struggle with that; not being able to forgive themselves. It's worth it, man, it really is. *You're* worth it. The next thing you gotta do is forgive others, it's not worth holding onto.

The old saying is: unforgiveness is like drinking poison and expecting the other person to die.

Make the decision to not hold on to things, to not hold grudges of unforgiveness or have unforgiveness in your heart. It's dangerous and deadly, not just for others but for you as well.

Pitfall 4

Anger

Anger is definitely a contributing factor to why there are so many people in prison, especially men, I believe, because at a critical split second, they didn't know how to control their anger. Their emotions got the best of them. I can't tell you how many men I talk to who told me if they had only taken a second, not a minute but a second, to think, it would've changed their whole situation and outcome. They let their anger control them.

What would've been useful would've been learning how to handle conflict instead. Growing up on Chicago's south side in the Robert Taylor Home projects, we didn't have conflict resolutions classes, we had fists and guns. That's how conflict usually got handled. It was wrong, but I never knew or was taught another way until I literally became a grown man.

I've had to attend Anger Management and Conflict Resolution classes. Unfortunately, it was not while I was growing up, it was actually when I was enrolled in a Modality program while I was incarcerated. A little late, but I did learn a few things.

I think everyone should take a Conflict Resolution class, people definitely could benefit, and it would help even with relationships, but I'm still finding out it only works when you work it.

Like myself, it's difficult for most men to communicate and express their feelings and be in touch with their emotions. Take a few seconds to try and be peaceful, that's what I try to do. It's hard, I struggle every day, I forget I need to do breathing exercises, I count to ten, take a minute, stop, check myself, or just go lay down. Honestly, sometimes it works and sometimes it doesn't. Regardless, it's always worth trying.

Pitfall 5
Jealousy

"For jealousy is the rage of a man: therefore, he will not spare in the day of vengeance" says Proverbs 6:34. When a person operates in jealousy, they lose the opportunity to celebrate, congratulate, or acknowledge an accomplishment of someone else who deserves it: for doing an excellent job. That's called being a "Hater." There's a saying, "Don't Hate, Congratulate." In the book of Ephesians 6:8 (NLT) it basically says: remember that the Lord will reward each one of us for the good we do, whether we are slaves or free." Jealousy is an ugly character trait that will not let you encourage others. Jealousy has been responsible for countless crimes committed.

In a fit of "jealous" rage, they say such and such happened. It makes people think crazy, suspicious, unrealistic, exaggerated thoughts. Many times, it's due to our own insecurities. And believe it or not, it's also part of fear.

If you recognize or have been told that you deal with jealousy, now is a good time to start being honest with yourself and work on doing better before it's too late.

Pitfall 6

Discouragement

"Hope deferred maketh the heart sick: but when the desire cometh, it is a tree of life." Proverbs 13:12 (KJV)

Everyone has to deal with discouragement at some point in their life. The problem is when you become overwhelmed with discouragement. When you allow it to overtake you, your outlook can become extremely dark. You lose hope.

You can't always tell when people are discouraged, but you can always tell when someone is encouraged or hopeful. You can hear it or see it in how they talk and how they live. When you see someone with low self-esteem, who's been verbally abused or is dealing with continual discouragement, they need encouragement immediately.

When it's you, that's feeling discouraged, try to speak life, light, love, or uplifting things about your situations. Positive thinking might not get you everything, but it will get you more than negative thinking.

Pitfall 7

Selfishness

I, I, I, Me, Me, Me.

Why do we put ourselves above and in front of others? We're born selfish. We have to be taught when we're young how to share our toys, food, and then as we age into adulthood, we have to learn how to share ourselves. By the time we get married, we should have already learned how to put someone before us. The problem is, we don't all learn that. Most of us miss it, every day. We put our jobs, friends, drinking, sports, money, ambitions, drugs, gambling, street life, really any and everything, before the things that really matter. If anyone calls us out on this or tells us we're being selfish, then we shut them out, either immediately or slowly. We don't want to hear that. We want to do what we want to do. But here's the deal on this; those people who are close enough to really see us, know us and know what they're talking about. We can't see it because we're in it. It's a blind spot for us. If I had listened every time my wife, or someone in my circle told me the truth instead of rejecting it, I'd never have fallen into my prison pit.

I was being selfish, not wanting to deal with pain. Like most men, I'm honestly still challenged about my selfishness by making excuses and not being present when I should be.

I'm an only child, a survivor by nature.

I always shared and gave, but unfortunately, I was taken advantage of too. I still can't see my selfishness at times, even though I have someone around who speaks the truth in love to me.

I'll give anyone the shirt off my back, I'll buy you something to eat if you're hungry, but when I want to do things my way… yep, I'm still working on it. We learn the first law of preservation is self-preservation. Maybe in certain situations we should re-think that, especially when it comes to the people we love and those who love us. Maybe it's better to give of ourselves than to hold back. Maybe that's why God says in John 15:13 "Greater love hath no man than this, that a man lay down his life for his friends."

So just like being selfish is natural, being unselfish needs to be learned. No matter what age.

When I was in Bible college, I had this epiphany...

Self spelled backwards adding a "H" in front of the "S" spells Flesh.

The flesh always wants what it wants. Today, I encourage you to learn to take the steps toward being unselfish, those who love you will appreciate you for it. Equally important is you'll be better for making the effort as well.

Pitfall 8

Bad Habits

We all have a few bad habits. The deal is to work on the bad habits and try to help keep and create more of the good habits. Acknowledging and appreciating our good habits will definitely help us as we work towards fulfilling our God-given purpose and destiny.

They say it takes 21 days to break bad habits and 21 days to develop good habits that will benefit us. Let's make a list. Making a good habit and a bad habit list will allow us to see some of the things we may need to focus on to be better people, for ourselves and for those who love us. Take some time to fill out the list of Good habits and Bad habits. Make sure you're keeping it real with yourself as you write, but don't be down on yourself, just be real with yourself.

Now here's where it really matters: your Good habits list has to be at least twice as long as your Bad habits list. If it's not, that's your current project to work on. After taking a good hard look at the list, work on eliminating as many bad habits as possible over time. There's an old saying that goes, "First we make our habits, then our habits make us."

If you're struggling with multiple bad habits that you know are not serving you in a good way, unhealthy mentally, physically, financially, or emotionally, if possible, talk to a professional or someone you really trust and can confide in.

I personally side with small steps lead to great victories. How do you get rid of bad habits? The answer to that is: one bad habit at a time. The same is true for the saying of "How do you eat an elephant?" The answer is one bite at a time.

Good Habits   Bad Habits

_____   _____

_____   _____

_____   _____

_____   _____

_____   _____

_____   _____

_____   _____

Pitfall 9

Regret

Everyone struggles with having done something we wish we could take back or have another chance to do over and make better choices. That's regret, it's impossible to go through life without it. The things we've said to others that we can never take back, something we did that can't be undone.

Sadly, we can never take back or change things once they've been done. I've never met anyone living a "Regret-free" life, but I have met people who are intentional about their decisions. My mother was like that. When she made up her mind to give up drugs, that was it for her, she never looked back. She regretted the years she had been using drugs, but she refused to live in regret, it was like she started her whole life over.

That's really what regret is, looking back. She told me she wanted to move out of her neighborhood, I immediately flew back to Chicago, rented a moving truck, and moved her into a high rise for seniors in downtown Chicago. It was the first time in over thirty years I had seen my mom sober and drug free. She was so happy. I was so happy and proud of her. Her whole life changed when she made up her mind and never looked back. No more regret, she started truly living her best life. My wife asked her one day what happened, what made her stop using drugs after all those years. She told her she got tired of living that kind of life, she told her that she got down on her knees and asked God to take it away, take away the taste and the desire for heroin. She had tried and failed many times before, but this time was different. This time was it; she had made her mind up to quit. She started traveling with my wife and I, along with my mother-in-law, it would be the four of us doing so much together for the first time in our lives, doing all kinds of things she'd never done before, and it was really beautiful to see her living like that. To set the record straight I'd like to state, that real men do cry. I can't count how many times I've cried as I wrote this book and especially times when I think of my brave, beautiful mother. Never be afraid or feel that only the weak shed tears. Truthfully after I was released from prison it took almost two years for me to cry. No matter what was said to me, about me, whatever comments, or rejection I faced; I felt nothing. I believe that was because I had insulated myself, buried my emotions as a way to protect myself from those around me but also from seriously letting my walls down and falling apart amongst the other inmates. I was grieving internally from my actions and the devastation I caused my wife and countless others. What finally brought my emotional release was interesting. While I was incarcerated my wife and I decided to put the marriage on hold and just remain friends. She'd finished Bible college and by this time was working on her Doctorate in Christian Theology, she'd started speaking and conducting workshops and I was excited for her, cheering for her on the sidelines. After my release, I was blessed to finally attend one of her major speaking events. I was stunned. She was brilliant and did so well, I was so proud of her. When we left and got in the car to head home, I just broke down in tears, I couldn't stop, I couldn't even talk. She didn't know what was wrong, she kept asking me and started holding me, trying to console me, then she started crying with me. Finally, I was able to say to her that I think I was crying because now I was able to see her do in person what she'd been telling me she did over the phone or in a letter or a picture. She had kept going, God hadn't let my incarceration hold her back, she didn't deserve that. Man, I tell you it broke me down to see her thrive in person, I was really happy for her after all I had put her through. Later, I realized I had actually been grieving for decades from the trauma and abuse I had encountered decades earlier. Since then, and before my release, I started my healing journey through ministry, counseling, and intentional therapy. I'm still enrolled voluntarily in therapy for a healthier mental and emotional existence. I think it's honestly a lifetime process and commitment, but that's another story.

Back to my mom, after getting clean, she lived a full life like I was saying before, she started living a Christian, drug free, sober life, one she dedicated to Jesus Christ her Lord and Savior, until the day she passed away. She was there when I took my first breath and I was there holding her hand when she took her last breath.I pray she's resting in peace and power.

She taught us the importance of our decisions and actions, she taught us how regret was a pit and that whatever we do will create an outcome; this is called "Cause and Effect."

Pitfall 10

Desperation

They say desperate people do desperate things. Sometimes we move ahead of God, we try to fix our problems by reacting instead of listening to The Holy Spirit, our families, friends, business partners, and even our gut instincts. We need to pray or even just wait and see instead of making impulsive decisions or moving ahead of God, this takes patience. A desperate person is not usually a patient person.

Usually, not always, we have options to utilize, to keep us from being in desperate situations. Practice patience, it's also one of the fruits of the spirit.

Pitfall 11

Immaturity

When we lack the ability to handle situations in a mature way, we can stumble into severe repercussions.

I saw men daily in prison handle certain situations immaturely, not being able to cope or deal from a place of maturity. I still see it now in men I meet almost daily, and unfortunately, honestly, at times, even in myself. I learned in therapy and counseling that a lot of that has to do with the trauma that individuals experienced in their lives at a young age where they become stunted due to abuse, whether it was physically violent, emotional, verbal, or the big one— sexual.

We all know about a person's IQ—Intelligence Quotient, but what we don't hear enough about is the EQ— Emotional Quotient, which is the ability to understand, use, and manage emotions.

I've really been able to see the immaturity in my own life, through the extensive counseling and therapy I've been enrolled in for the past few years. In the past, men talking about their emotions and problems was straight taboo forbidden. Nowadays, it's becoming far more acceptable. I've had to learn to accept and embrace extensive therapy and counseling, in addition to consistent Pastoral accountability with my Spiritual Dad. All coupled with my relationship with God as part of my own healing from childhood personal traumas of physical, verbal, and sexual abuses I experienced.

Age doesn't equal maturity. I highly recommend anyone who has dealt with any of these abuses to get some genuine help in the form of professional therapy or counseling. It's worth it on so many levels, and you can't afford to care about what somebody else thinks, that's part of being mature.

There's so much information out now from studies to research that show proof of how negatively impacted the brain is from trauma and abuse. The manifestation is inevitable, and it varies from person to person. Everyone deals with trauma and abuse differently. As hard as it is to deal with, I've had to learn and accept the fact that the abuse that I experienced wasn't my fault. The same is true for you and your childhood traumas.

All pain is not the same, yet we never, ever have the right to judge anyone else's pain. Just know that whatever happened to you: it wasn't your fault, as hard as it is to deal with…

Pitfall 12

Rebellion

To purposely go against our supportive families, good systems, uplifting organizations, or even a belief that's beneficial can close us off from endless possibilities. Rebellion.

Often as men, we don't like to be told what to do, we like to think we know what we're doing, we have it all together, but sometimes we're literally going against the grain when we embrace that my way or the highway mindset. Rebellion.

Sometimes people revolt against someone or a system when they don't agree or understand it. Be sure to check yourself first and understand your reasoning and motivation for going against something. Always consider the consequences of your decisions when and if you still choose to rebel. Count the cost, it really may not even be worth it.

Pitfall 13

Irresponsibility

Everyone can't be responsible; but anyone can be irresponsible. When you are responsible, people can count on you, rely on you, and depend on you in a good way, I'm not saying be a pushover. Whether it's at home, among friends, or at work, you want to show you can handle the responsibilities that have been given to you. Especially in your relationships.

A reputation of being irresponsible is hard to shake off, basically because it describes the behavior and the way you do things: irresponsibly. Irresponsibility is part of your character, and lack of integrity.

The funny thing is, being responsible is the exact opposite, it will motivate you to follow through on your word, allow you to be dependable, reliable, and probably more than anything; it'll show you as a man of integrity.

Pitfall 14

Ignorance

The definition of ignorance is described as the lack of knowledge or lack of information. Some things we should just know.

In prison, when you come in for the first time, they call you "Green" meaning you're new and ignorant. Which is true, yet it's not a good thing.

Who really wants to be ignorant—lacking knowledge and info in any situation? Nobody. But especially not in a situation where your life is on the line daily. You have to learn the ropes real quick, if not; there may be problems.

A family member told me "To be aware is to be alive." As a husband, the head of your household, a man, a friend, or as a family member, it's so important to understand ignorance is not bliss, it can be dangerous, sinful, and even deadly. Do not be ignorant, be informed.

God says in 2 Corinthians 2:11, "I will not have you ignorant to the devices of the enemy." Know yourself, get to know your God, and always know your enemies because they (he) knows you.

Pitfall 15

Fear

Fear can be crippling and has kept people from fulfilling their purpose and destiny, this type of fear can be called fear of success. It's been shown that fear has literally paralyzed people physically and mentally, when confronted in certain situations.

Just know that whatever you do, fear is not our friend, it's the opposite of faith. I've seen people do some seriously crazy things out of straight up fear.

There are hundreds of Bible scriptures on fear. God is always telling us to be courageous and do not fear! This particular pit alone is enough to write and fill a whole book. I'll stop here, knowing like everyone else; you've had your own experiences and are able to identify with fear in some form or fashion. It is one of the most common pits in life.

Pitfall 16

Rejection

To disregard, to minimize, to not allow an opening or acceptance of an individual, group, club, etc., that's the definition of rejection.

The enemy of our souls wants people to feel rejected, to feel less than, whether it's low self-esteem, a sense of worthlessness, not fitting in, not feeling appreciated, not thinking we're good enough, or even not like others. All of that adds to a person feeling and dealing with rejection. I honestly didn't see my rejection issues until I came to terms with how I was conceived. I'm an only child, my mother loved me with everything in her, and I know she did the best she could, but I was conceived in a rape. The ultimate rejection. She still did one of the hardest things in her life, which was making the choice to not only give birth to me, but she chose to keep me. I remember her telling me something I'll never forget. She was close to death, she looked at me and said, "I never thought I could love somebody the way I love you." Someone might think that's just a mother's love, but I'll never know how much it took for her to look at the reminder of the worst day of her life and love it like nothing else.

I love my mother with all my heart to this day and am eternally grateful to her for making the choice she made to bring me into the world. I honestly have dealt with depression almost as long as I can remember, even suicidal at times. But the sacrifice made for me to be here always outweighs thoughts of not being here.

All my life, I've dealt with rejection because of this, but I make the choice to press through it every day. I challenge people to "Reject Rejection."

You're good enough, you matter, but most importantly— you're accepted by your Heavenly Father.

Pitfall 17

Criticism

If it's not constructive, we cross over into being judgmental of people. Circumstances and situations can teach us how to criticize in a healthy way. When criticism is done in a good way, that's what's called constructive criticism, but that's not where the pitfall is, the pitfall is when we let it start to destroy us, either by giving out so much criticism, or being the receiver of excessive criticism. The Bible literally says in the book of Matthew 7:1(KJV) "that in the same way we judge others we will be judged." So, let's be careful when we feel that we have the right to criticize others or we're the receivers of excessive criticism, either way; this pit is extremely damaging.

Pitfall 18
Perversion

Many people deal with the spirit of perversion; it is a vice that our enemy uses to keep people in bondage. Perverting, altering, changing, distorting something; changing anything from its original healthy natural origin to an unhealthy unnatural origin. Basically, turning it into something negative and wrong, from how something was said to what people thought was said.

This was God's word to Adam and Eve not to eat of the tree of knowledge of good and evil. Satan told Eve that God said they should not eat of the tree because God knew they would be as God. He perverted the truth. Whether it's friends, family, or associates, the enemy will pervert what was said to mislead, misguide, and misdirect words to fit their twisted agenda.

In prison this practice is also common and jokingly called Inmate.com, where any and every kind of rumor can be started and spread like wildfire, however its usually wrong with only a touch of truth but it is now completely distorted. Inmate.com is full of lies and gossip. Be mindful to what the ears hear, what the eyes see and what the mouth says. Definitely work to guard them all from any type of perversion.

Pitfall 19
Pornography

Men are visual individuals, and if the vision is not healthy, it can defile and destroy. The porn business is a billion-dollar business due to vision and what the eye gate is watching. Countless men from all walks of life deal with porn addictions. An unhealthy vision is detrimental to a man who's dealing with a pornography addiction. It will require accountability, focus, and most importantly—how healthy you see yourself and your future.

Overcoming addiction is possible with true intentionality, accountability, and putting in the incredibly challenging work to do it. The stats on this addictive pit among men is staggering. Whether for men in church or out of church, it's a dangerous, scandalous, evil, seducing pit.

Mark 10:27 says And Jesus looking upon them saith, "With men it is impossible, but not with God: for with God all things are possible."

Pitfall 20

Alcohol Abuse

Alcohol abuse has been around since the beginning of time but watch it. Can drinking be okay if done in moderation? The jury is still out on that one, it depends on who you're asking.

People drink excessively, abuse alcohol, and, honestly, it's socially acceptable. However, there are those who drink to forget the past of pain and hurt, an escapism, avoiding disappointment and all that comes with it. But the problems are still there after you sober up. It's a choice to look into; confront your alcohol issues associated with any fears and uncertainties head on, or you can get the help you need. There is no right or wrong way to get sober, it's just a matter of which way is best for you. Those who love you will appreciate you making the choice to sober up.

Pitfall 21

Drug Abuse

Drug abuse, like any addiction, can be hereditary. Like drinking, people can use drugs for escapism. With the rise of the abuse of prescription painkillers such as opioids, the game has definitely changed. The abuse of opioid drugs is still climbing, having almost surpassed the crack epidemic of the 90s. As I've already said, my beautiful precious mother was a heroin addict for over 30 years. I know firsthand on both sides how it is watching drug abuse run wild in someone else's life, to using myself. When I was 10 years old, I started using marijuana, and on a couple of occasions, an older cousin who was an addict shot me up with heroin. I struggled for the majority of my life. That's how I know firsthand how destructive drug abuse is, from seeing it and being it. Drug abuse has ruined men, families, friendships, careers, communities, cities, even nations. Find healthy ways to deal with anything that tries to control you. Counseling, therapy, AA, NA, SOP, Pastoral overseeing, and definitely prayer are a few different ways of treatment that could help lead to a free new you.

Pitfall 22

Prejudice

Being prejudiced is a seriously detestable, sometimes taught, behavior. It's been around forever, and we're still seeing, lately, more and more. It's usually against a race of people. It can start from so many places, family, friends, culture, history, ignorance, or even, unfortunately, an experience. When individuals don't know someone or something, or don't understand or can't relate to one another, a pre-judgment against one another can arise. I see this daily, I live it, especially being a black man in America right now, and, of course, while I was incarcerated. Unfortunately, I honestly didn't learn firsthand about systemic racism until I was in my forties. I will tell you it is absolutely a choice though.

I love all people. I kick it with all races. We treat each other with love and respect. I wasn't taught to be prejudiced and have chosen to this day not to be prejudiced. Black, Asian,

Italian, Jewish, White, etc. On any given day, that's who you will find around me, and I will offer no apologies.

Here's the thing, while incarcerated it was the same way, I got along with mostly everybody. Don't get me wrong I definitely had my share of problems with people during my time, but it was usually situational not racial. I don't know how we can always get along, but there's a Bible verse where it seems like God knows it's a challenge because He says in Romans 12:18 "If it be possible, as much as leith in you, live peaceably with all men" You see He says "if" right? Enough said.

When you see 28 Pitfalls in prison, it can show up through organized racism in groups, clubs, dorms, and even in the chapel. I'd like to see us all treated equal, as simple as that. Equal.

We're really something when we all stand together. I encourage you to consciously choose not to be prejudiced, again, like so many other things… it's a mind over matter choice.

Pitfall 23

Hatred

Hatred is sometimes taught in families, groups, institutions, and life in general. If hatred is fed, it can do plenty of damage. It can and will produce a horrible attitude, filth in the heart and in the mouth, it's hard to hide and easy to see. People hate people, and even themselves, and they don't know why. Whether it's because of an ethnicity, political party, community, color, race, religion, gender, or economic status. Hate is a strong negative reaction or feeling toward someone, sometimes considered an enemy. This is one particular pitfall that seems to live inside of people and unfortunately they can be totally unaware of it. This one day I felt I had hate in me. I was mad and feeling hateful. I was mad at people, myself and everyone I even thought was not doing things the way I thought they be should doing them, especially how I thought they should be doing things in regard to me. Go ahead laugh, shake your head at me but you know how that is too right? It's ok, we all do. Well my wife was trying to get me back on track to thinking right by being positive and encouraging me to shake it off by telling me to stop being angry at people and named a few people she said she knew I was angry at, people on my crap list to put it mildly. After she finished with a few names I just looked at her while I was smoking my cigarette, I blew out smoke and calmly said to her "you forgot a lot more people." Then I told her something. I told her that earlier that same day, I had actually made a mental list in my head of people who was on that crap list. I don't know who else does that but on this day I actually did. Imagine that, a grown man with a crap list. I can laugh at it now but not that day. I want to tell you that day I walked around mumbling, talking crazy, snapping at people and honestly spent my day being hateful. It was a waste. I came in, took a shower, put my pajamas on then did what I knew I was suppose to do...I got in the bed refusing to spill my hatred on to another person. I don't know what I learned that day but I read what God says in The Message version of The Bible in Proverbs 4:23-27 "Keep vigilant watch over your heart; that's where life starts. Don't talk out of both sides of your mouth; avoid careless banter, white lies, and gossip.

Keep your eyes straight ahead; ignore all sideshow distractions.

Watch your step, and the road will stretch out smooth before you.

Look neither right nor left; leave evil in the dust." We have to guard our hearts, otherwise we let stuff in that could mess us up for real.

God makes us a promise in the book of Ezekiel 36:26-28

"I'll give you a new heart, put a new spirit in you. I'll remove the stone heart from your body and replace it with a heart that's God-willed, not self-willed. I'll put my Spirit in you and make it possible for you to do what I tell you and live by my commands."

Simply put to me this means a heart that's stone is already dead, but a heart of flesh is alive. So be mindful to your feelings and emotions. Hate what God hates and love what God loves. I made up this acronym about what the letters that spell out HATE really mean:

H-horrible A-angry T-terrible E-evil. Hate is a strong negative reaction or feeling toward someone, sometimes considered an enemy. Hate what God hates and love what God loves. Love wins, always.

Pitfall 24

Mocking

When a person is mocked, scorned, poked fun at, minimized or disregarded, made fun of, disrespected, or even made to be a laughingstock, etc. there's gonna be trouble. The Bible says "Be not deceived; God will not be mocked: for whatsoever a man soweth, that shall he reap also" Galatians 6:7.

Nobody likes to be made fun of, minimized, cruelly laughed at, be the center of negative jokes, or receive negative mocking attention. Made to feel like your existence is a disgraceful joke. That's one of the easiest ways to get into a fight in prison, and be killed for that matter. At this point, "Manhood" is at stake. When a grown man in prison is belittled by another grown man, in front of other men; the EGO's (Edging God Out) take over, all common sense goes out the door, this I know firsthand. However, I can tell you this; try not to be the one mocking others, if you are the one being mocked; keep in mind what's at stake at the end of the day and choose your reaction wisely.

Pitfall 25

Impatience

Impatience is a tricky pit. It means to have or show a tendency to be quickly irritated or provoked, restless, or too eager. This one is very personal and still a major pitfall for me, and plenty of others I've seen. I have a problem with sometimes moving ahead of God, being impatient, and yes, it usually goes haywire or downhill, because I'm still trying to do things my way. Whatever it is, I want it now; I want it yesterday. I'll try to make something happen before I see it happening. I'm learning new ways of being still, like waiting awhile, but at the end of the day; I'm still very impatient. It's hard, I'm not sure how well I'm doing with this pit, but I'm aware of it. If I think people are talking to slow for me, I don't mean to cut them off or interrupt, but I do. I'm working on it. If there's an opportunity that looks good, there's a fifty-fifty chance that I'll wait, weigh it out, pray about it, or I'll jump right in. Yep, jumping in is still an option, and it shouldn't be.

I know, pray for me, man, these are real life pitfalls.

I admit I mess up and interrupt still, but I'm catching myself more, I'll apologize, acknowledge my impatience, then be quiet. Sometimes.

I'll tell you this one thing I do know for sure...we are all works in progress, masterpieces in the making, no matter how hard it gets.

Pitfall 26

Adultery

Adultery is a straight up act of unfaithfulness in marriage that happens when one of the marriage partners voluntarily engages in sexual intercourse, intimacy, oral sex, phone sex, or sexting with a person other than their spouse.

The Biblical standard for marriage is a monogamous relationship. Commit to a lifetime commitment to each other and God. Adultery has been around since the beginning of time, and it has affected nations of people's sexual immorality, then and now. King David was a man after God's own heart but got caught up with this one that turned from adultery to murder. From my own personal painful experience of the hurt, pain, suffering, and heartbreak I caused, I say avoid this pitfall at all costs. It's not worth it.

As men, we need to not only be very careful but extremely intentional about this. We are better than this, but even more important, our wives and families deserve better and are worth so much more than this.

Pitfall 27

Lack of Discipline

When I looked up what the word discipline means, it said Discipline comes from the Latin word "disco," which means to learn or get to know a direct kind of acquaintance with something or someone. When you don't have discipline, it shows up in different key areas of your life. I look at discipline like a tool used for training yourself for the win. What happens when you don't have it or lack it? You will not follow through, you will not be consistent, you'll have patterns of incompleteness, you'll make excuses.

Let me just say this; not having discipline is the pits. Take discipline seriously. Successful discipline results in a life pleasing to God. We should learn this one early in life through organized sports, clubs, school or really just about any structured activity but sometimes we miss it. Developing and applying discipline can really help us persevere through a lot of life's ups and downs, but the lack of discipline will stagnate us. It's not too late, you got this.

Pitfall 28

Lying

God tells us that the truth will set us free. Whether it's out of fear, just being dumb, or whatever the poor excuse is, people will lie for whatever reason, thinking it's to get out of trouble or whatever, but the bottom line is this….a lie deceives ourselves and others. Period.

Some people lie to be accepted or liked. I was a big liar growing up, I dealt with so much shame. I thought I was covering up how bad my life really was. I called it exaggerating, but no; I was lying. One of the biggest conclusions I've come to with this pitfall is so simple: I never want to be perceived as a liar. Being a liar is disgraceful. We have to believe and accept the truth is good enough, it's as simple as that. Nothing more, nothing less—the truth is enough.

BONUS

Pitfall 29

Not Loving Yourself

Many people deal with acceptance issues, whether it's from childhood rejection, low self-esteem, loneliness, focusing on what's wrong instead of what's right, or some other form of dysfunction. Not loving or valuing yourself can lead to people joining gangs, clubs, and groups they really shouldn't be part of. Being part of something makes them feel a sense of family or belonging. My situation growing up was no different, you are searching for something to fill a void, you'll have both men and women looking for love and acceptance in all the wrong places. I have dealt with this for a big part of my life, I'm learning how important it is to keep my standards, set healthy boundaries as I learn more about loving the man I'm becoming and not feel like I have to earn love from others.

Everybody deep down wants to be liked and accepted, even to the point of losing themselves trying to be liked or accepted by others. I used to not understand what it meant when I heard people, honestly it was mostly women say "You have to love yourself first." I was like what kind of daytime talk show fluff is that! But I'm definitely learning how important and what it is to really love yourself. I challenge you to get in the mirror daily and tell yourself *God loves me and I'm enough*. **If God is for us, who can be against us? Romans 8:31(KJV**

After Thoughts

Now that you've finished reading *28 Pitfalls of a Man*, my prayer is that you found it helpful and enlightening as you take on the challenges or even being aware of what it'll take in overcoming these particular daily pitfalls you'll face. There's plenty more that you'll face in life. You probably already recognize some I didn't talk about that you've already faced. We all have to face them. One of the most important things we can do as adults, regardless whether you're in prison or not, is to take responsibility for our actions and never blame others. It's not someone else's fault, it's called "Manning Up," own it, learn from it, then move on. They say doing the same thing over and over and expecting different results is the definition of insanity. That's why it's definitely okay to pick up your copy of *28 Pitfalls of a Man* as often as you need to. Especially when you need to get refreshed or refocused as part of your maintenance as opposed to your repair.

I try not to tell people what to do, I just offer my experience along with any information that could help. I would say if your pit right now is a real physical prison, then most definitely use one hundred percent of the time you're there wisely. This will allow you to not serve time, but make the time serve you in ways that help you to be productive and purposeful. Whether your sentence is a year and a day or life; get new. New attitude, new mind set, new goals, new focus, new purpose, new good habits, new motivation, a new plan along with a completely new way of living. While I was incarcerated I read close to three hundred books and journaled almost everyday, trust me I'm not bragging because prior to my incarceration I would barely read a few books a year and thought journaling was for poets. After I was released my wife and I made it a couples goal to not only continue to read, but read at least a book together a month. Our own little book club. That doesn't sound like a big deal I know, but making the time and even staying committed to follow through on that is still really challenging.

I say that to say anything we really want to do, we usually make a way to do it. Make a way to be better to yourself, especially make your mental self-care a priority.

As a black man I've become more aware and open to diversity, culture, race and gender issues, specifically by sitting in on Diversity lectures or workshops my wife conducts. I've discovered that I can't be embarrassed embracing my self-care these days.

The statistics from NAMI- National Alliance on Mental Illness for Blacks is jaw dropping. According to the Health and Human Services Office of Minority Health, Black adults in the U.S. are more likely than white adults to report persistent symptoms of emotional distress, such as sadness, hopelessness and feeling like everything is an effort. Black adults living below the poverty line are more than twice as likely to report serious psychological distress than those with more financial security.

Despite the needs, only one in three Black adults who need mental health care receive it. According to the American Psychiatric Association's Mental Health Facts for African Americans guide, they are also:

- Less likely to receive guideline-consistent care

- Less frequently included in research

- More likely to use emergency rooms or primary care (rather than mental health specialists).

This is just another reason of why it's so important to get the help needed. Whatever your race may be, keep in mind it's not your business to worry about what other people think about your self-care, remember at the end of the day it not only benefits everyone around you, but at the heart of it, it's really for you.

I wrote this with my wife, as a way to encourage myself daily, then we decided to share it. The key is not just to avoid the pitfalls but learn to recognize, confront, and overcome them. This takes a lot of effort and diligence, but not dealing with these and any other pitfalls can potentially rob us of our destiny and purpose. I pray the physical prison, mental prison, or emotional prison you face will be a wakeup call or just a pit stop along the way to your destiny and purpose. I always wish I could change the things I've done wrong, the people I hurt by the bad decisions I've made, but I can't, nobody can, the regret and remorse are real. I know and tell others from my firsthand experience that childhood hidden secrets must be revealed in order for people to heal. What I can do now is exactly what I'm telling you; I can share my mistakes with others in hopes that it may help them to not make the same mistakes I've already made. If we knew better, we'd do better, we live and we learn. Like I said at the beginning of the book: no one wants to be remembered for the worse things they've ever done on the worst days of their lives. Remember, good, better, best, never let it rest until your good becomes your better and your better becomes your best. Now, let's go live the life God created us to live.

Salvation Prayer

Insert your first and last name

_____Salvation Prayer

_____Today's date

Believe, breath, and repeat the following: I'm still breathing, it's not too late. No more feeling unworthy, rejected, or ashamed, like I don't belong, or I made too many mistakes. I was chosen before the foundation of the earth. I'm a loved man of God by my Father in heaven who loves me more than I'll ever know. I Invite You, King Jesus into my heart by speaking this prayer: Father God, I confess I am a sinner, I ask You to forgive me for my sins, I believe Jesus died for me and rose for me. I ask Him to come into my heart, I make Jesus my Lord and My Savior. In Jesus' name, I pray, amen.

Congratulations welcome to the family!

Spend time reading, praising, studying, worshipping, and meditating in God's word.

It's not about religion, it's about your relationship with your Father in heaven who wants to spend time with you, as you get to know Him more, He wants to have a real relationship with you, like never before. It's a new day.

Romans 10:9 KJV says "That if thou shalt confess with thy mouth the Lord Jesus, and shalt believe in thine heart that God hath raised him from the dead, thou shalt be saved."

Talk It Over

28 Pitfalls Of A Man

_____

_____

_____

_____

_____

_____

_____

_____

_____

_____

_____

_____

_____

_____

_____

_____

_____

_____

_____

_____

_____

_____

_____

_____

_____

_____

_____

_____

_____

_____

_____

_____

_____

_____

_____

_____

_____

_____

_____

_____

_____

_____

_____

_____

_____

_____

_____

_____

_____

_____

_____

_____

_____

_____

_____

_____

_____

_____

_____

_____

_____

_____

_____

_____

_____

_____

_____

_____

_____

_____

_____

_____

_____

_____

_____

_____

_____

_____

_____

_____

_____

_____

_____

_____

_____

_____

_____

_____

28 Pitfalls Of A Man

_____

_____

_____

_____

_____

_____

_____

_____

_____

_____

_____

_____

_____

_____

_____

_____

_____

_____

_____

_____

_____

_____

_____

_____

_____

_____

_____

_____

_____

_____

_____

_____

_____

_____

_____

_____

_____

_____

_____

_____

_____

_____

_____

_____

_____

_____

_____

_____

_____

_____

_____

_____

_____

_____

_____

_____

_____

_____

_____

_____

_____

_____

_____

_____

_____

_____

_____

_____

_____

_____

_____

_____

_____

_____

28 Pitfalls Of A Man

_____

_____

_____

_____

_____

_____

_____

_____

_____

_____

_____

_____

_____

_____

_____

_____

_____

_____

Hurt people, hurt people. Healed people, heal people.

~ Author Unknown

Acknowledgements

I would like to acknowledge my inner circle of family and friends; Dr. Latera & Dr. Glenda Akiens, my spiritual parents for almost two decades. Thank you for your unconditional love and encouragement, helping me get through Bible college, the sacrifices you both made, your faithfulness and unwavering support for me. I watched you, Dad, go through an extremely difficult health journey with Glenda (my spiritual Mom) right by your side, yet every other month during my incarceration, you both came nine hours to see me, faithfully. Even hours after your treatments. It would choke me up, I'll never forget that. I'm forever grateful to you both. Y'all are my hearts since meeting in Celebration to eternity. I love the two of you so much.

Maurice McClain, my brother from another mother for almost three decades. Man, I could drop real tears thinking about how much you've grown spiritually in your relationship with God. Not comparing yourself or trying to keep up with anybody else, you've put in the work, and it shows. I can never repay you for all the love and support you've shown me.

We are brothers for life. I'm eternally grateful to you for standing with me through it all. I love you, Bro.

My Aunt Dear, Misky, Ann, Ray, Dawn Marie, Rosadely, Lou, Pastors EJ & Delia, The Johnsons, The Wrights, The Nixons, The Carters, Pastors Tom & Jane, Mike, Steve, and Dr. Karyn, I'll never forget the kindness, love, and support you all showed from fasting to finances to opportunities. May God reward you all for the faithfulness you've all shown. To W.R. you are without a doubt a true stand-up man and a straight shooter, who I consider as my accountability Coach. You're leading me and countless others by your example-I appreciate you. Dave, you've taught and trained me in broadcasting and media without holding back anything. They say when the student is ready the teacher will appear, you came into my life at the appointed time and helped me cultivate a God given gift I didn't even know I had, with my voice. You're a great teacher thank you man. Pastor Norbey your prison ministry and generous love for God shows in everything you are and do, I along with many others are definitely recipients of that, thank you forever. To all the saints of God, my family, and all of my friends, thank you for all the prayers and continual support. God bless you all.

It's not easy to apologize.

It's not easy to begin over.

It's not easy to be unselfish.

It's not easy to admit error.

It's not easy facing a stare.

It's not easy to be charitable.

It's not easy to keep trying.

It's not easy to be considerate.

It's not easy to avoid mistakes.

-Author Unknown

About the Author

28 Pitfalls was inspired after a series of mental, emotional, and spiritual setbacks, coupled with unresolved childhood abusive trauma that attributed to Rodney's incarceration. It was during his time in prison while working on himself, his faith, helping others, along with preparing for his own redemption back into society, that *28 Pitfalls of a Man* started. He acknowledges it was the forgiveness and faithfulness of God that helped him persevere throughout his incarceration. During his incarceration, as a team leader, Rodney taught his wife's Personal enrichment courses in the Re-entry program, while also teaching job training skills. In the Education Dept, he was an Education Orderly helping prepare men to receive their GED's, along with tutoring several subjects. He also worked as a Chapel Orderly in the Chapel. A few years prior to his incarceration after partnering with his wife in several successful businesses for over twenty years at the age of 43 years old, Rodney pursued and obtained his high school diploma. During his incarceration, he received his Associate of Arts, Bachelor of Theology, and Master of Arts Theology from International College of Ministry in Winter Park,

Florida. Even though it's been several years ago since his incarceration Rodney is dedicated to serving alongside those involved in Restorative Justice practices as an active member of various statewide and national organizations. He is the founder of Redemption 100, a non-profit organization committed to prison reform and assisting those formerly incarcerated, to navigate successfully back into society. Rodney and his family honor faith-based values and enjoy spending time together with loved ones.

Made in the USA
Columbia, SC
03 March 2023

13219350R00054